Building the Dream Team

Workbook

Julia A. Royston

ROYSTON
Publishing

BK Royston Publishing
P. O. Box 4321
Jeffersonville, IN 47131
502-802-5385
http://www.bkroystonpublishing.com
bkroystonpublishing@gmail.com

Published and Cover Design by: BK Royston Publishing LLC

ISBN-13: 978-1502818454
ISBN-10: 1502818450

Printed in the United States of America

Acknowledgement

I thank my Lord and Savior Jesus Christ for giving me another opportunity to introduce more people to you. I thank you that you have entrusted this gift to me. Lord, let your Spirit move through this book to the people who will read it.

To my husband, Brian K. Royston, the love of my life for loving and cheering me on so much that I can be and do all that God has placed in me. I love you...

To my Mom, who is a great support and to my Dad who is in heaven but, I know is proud of me and always encouraged me to go for it. Thanks to all of my family for their love and support.

A special thank you to Rev. and Mrs. Claude R. Royston for their love and support. Papa thank you for using your fine tooth comb to edit this book again.

I dedicate this book to every person in the world who is striving to build a dream team for ministry, business, a non-profit organization or a family.

Love, Julia A. Royston

Dedication

I dedicate this to every person who has ever felt alone while striving to make your dream come true.

I pray that you receive the courage to keep going, strength from God to keep growing and knowledge from the masters to keep knowing.

Your dream team is on the way and I trust that God give you the wisdom and discernment to know the difference between a scream and your dream team.

Introduction

This workbook accompanies the book "Building the Dream Team." The "Building the Dream Team" Workbook is designed to put down on paper the dream team that you would like to see in your business, organization or ministry. The bible says, "Write the Vision and Make it Plain." Habakkuk 2:2 (KJV)

The workbook and book are companions and complement each other. You will need to purchase the book "Building the Dream Team" to get the most benefit out of the workbook. The book, "Building the Dream Team" provides the definitions, descriptions and designates the guidelines for building a dream team.

Reading a book is wonderful but, there is something about writing down in your own handwriting your plans or ideas that makes them more real.

I have provided extra blank journal pages to make notes, write down other ideas or questions to ask later in another setting.

My desire is for you to be, do and have all that you have dreamed for your life. My other desire is that you fulfill your God given purpose in the earth.

It's time to 'go big or don't go at all.' Built correctly, the Dream Team will help to Transform the World!

Let's Build the Team!

Business Profile

Describe your business, organization or service that is in need of a
team?

_____

_____

_____

_____

_____

_____

_____

_____

_____

_____

_____

_____

_____

_____

_____

_____

_____

_____

_____

_____

_____

_____

_____

_____

Who are your current supporters or team members of the business, organization or service?

_____

_____

_____

_____

_____

_____

_____

_____

_____

_____

_____

_____

_____

_____

_____

_____

_____

_____

_____

_____

_____

_____

_____

_____

_____

_____

What services do the current team members or supports provide that benefits your business, organization or service?

_____

_____

_____

_____

_____

_____

_____

_____

_____

_____

_____

_____

_____

_____

_____

_____

_____

_____

_____

_____

_____

_____

_____

_____

_____

Why do you feel that you need an additional or different team than what you are currently working with? What are the benefits, results, assets or value that a new team will bring to your business, organization and services?

_____

_____

_____

_____

_____

_____

_____

_____

_____

_____

_____

_____

_____

_____

_____

_____

_____

_____

_____

_____

_____

_____

_____

Business or Organization Structure Profile

List the various roles, responsibilities or positions that you will need from your team. If you know job titles, provide them. If you only know a description of the duties you need performed, provide that as well.

_____

_____

_____

_____

_____

_____

_____

_____

_____

_____

_____

_____

_____

_____

_____

_____

_____

_____

_____

_____

_____

Leadership Profile of Business, Organization or Service

Describe your leadership style in specific terms.

_____

_____

_____

_____

_____

_____

_____

_____

_____

_____

_____

_____

_____

_____

_____

_____

_____

_____

_____

_____

_____

_____

_____

_____

_____

General Description or Profile of each of your organization's positions or roles in your business, organization or service

For example, Team Leader, Leadership Officers, Manufacturing Work Force, Administrative Officers

_____

_____

_____

_____

_____

_____

_____

_____

_____

_____

_____

_____

_____

_____

_____

_____

_____

_____

_____

_____

_____

_____

_____

_____

_____

_____

_____

What different types of teams does your business, organization or service need? For example, sales team, administrative team, research and development team, marketing team, social media team..

_____

_____

_____

_____

_____

_____

_____

_____

_____

_____

_____

_____

_____

_____

_____

_____

_____

_____

_____

_____

_____

_____

_____

_____

_____

Team Profile – Inner Circle – List the Members of Your Inner Circle

_____

_____

_____

_____

_____

_____

_____

_____

_____

_____

_____

_____

_____

_____

_____

_____

_____

_____

_____

_____

_____

_____

_____

_____

_____

_____

_____

Team Profile – Outer Circle – List the Members of your Outer Circle

_____

_____

_____

_____

_____

_____

_____

_____

_____

_____

_____

_____

_____

_____

_____

_____

_____

_____

_____

_____

_____

_____

_____

_____

_____

_____

Team Profile – Competitive Circle – List the Members of Your Competitive Circle

_____

_____

_____

_____

_____

_____

_____

_____

_____

_____

_____

_____

_____

_____

_____

_____

_____

_____

_____

_____

_____

_____

_____

_____

_____

_____

Team Profile – Galaxy and Beyond – Who do you want on your Galaxy and Beyond Team?

_____

_____

_____

_____

_____

_____

_____

_____

_____

_____

_____

_____

_____

_____

_____

_____

_____

_____

_____

_____

_____

_____

_____

_____

_____

_____

_____

_____

_____

_____

Team Member Personality Profile

Provide a general description or a list of descriptors of the personality type for your team members and their roles.

_____
_____
_____
_____
_____
_____
_____
_____
_____
_____
_____
_____
_____
_____
_____
_____
_____
_____
_____
_____
_____
_____
_____
_____
_____
_____
_____

Team Members

List how many team members that you desire on your team. Be specific about the role, position and duties of each team member.

_____

_____

_____

_____

_____

_____

_____

_____

_____

_____

_____

_____

_____

_____

_____

_____

_____

_____

_____

_____

_____

_____

_____

_____

_____

Team Member Recruiting Strategy

Where will your team members come from? What recruiting methods will you utilize to locate team members? For example, references, other friends, family, social media, newspaper, head hunter..

_____

_____

_____

_____

_____

_____

_____

_____

_____

_____

_____

_____

_____

_____

_____

_____

_____

_____

_____

_____

_____

_____

_____

Team Diversity

Provide a statement or profile on your team's diversified personality, skill, mindset or ability. How will your team be diversified? For example, by sex, ability, personality, background.. What are the different traits that you are looking for to make your team diversified?

_____

_____

_____

_____

_____

_____

_____

_____

_____

_____

_____

_____

_____

_____

_____

_____

_____

_____

_____

_____

_____

_____

_____

_____

_____

Team Parameters

Guidelines, Rules or Regulations for your Team (s) Members and their roles, positions and tasks.

_____
_____
_____
_____
_____
_____
_____
_____
_____
_____
_____
_____
_____
_____
_____
_____
_____
_____
_____
_____
_____
_____
_____
_____
_____
_____

Team Leader Parameters

What are the Parameters surrounding the Team Leader? What are the guidelines, limits or borders surround the various team leaders?

_____

_____

_____

_____

_____

_____

_____

_____

_____

_____

_____

_____

_____

_____

_____

_____

_____

_____

_____

_____

_____

_____

_____

_____

_____

Team Tools Needed to get the Job Done

What are the tools that your team will need to get the job done?
Technology, equipment, supplies, telecommunications..

_____

_____

_____

_____

_____

_____

_____

_____

_____

_____

_____

_____

_____

_____

_____

_____

_____

_____

_____

_____

_____

_____

_____

_____

_____

Team Development

What training, workshops, software or conferences will your team need to attend, receive or determined to be and do their best?

_____

_____

_____

_____

_____

_____

_____

_____

_____

_____

_____

_____

_____

_____

_____

_____

_____

_____

_____

_____

_____

_____

_____

_____

_____

Celebrations for Your Team

What type of celebrations will you have for your team? Use this space as a planning guide for your team celebrations. Plan a celebration each month, quarter, bi-annually or annually.

_____

_____

_____

_____

_____

_____

_____

_____

_____

_____

_____

_____

_____

_____

_____

_____

_____

_____

_____

_____

_____

_____

_____

_____

One Team Ends and Another Begins

Every organization needs a back –up plan or plan B. What if the current team walked away from you today, what would be your plan B? Are there organizations that you know of that could handle the roles, positions or tasks that your current team take care of? Who are they? If you don't know these organizations yet, what would are the immediate needs, short term needs and/or long-term needs?

Team Back-up Plan or Plan B

_____

_____

_____

_____

_____

_____

_____

_____

_____

_____

_____

_____

_____

_____

_____

_____

_____

_____

_____

_____

Organizations that can handle your team's responsibilities in an emergency? List three to five organizations that outsource and can mimic your team's abilities.

_____

_____

_____

_____

_____

_____

_____

_____

_____

_____

_____

_____

What are the Immediate Needs from a New Team or Outsourcing Organization?

_____

_____

_____

_____

_____

_____

_____

_____

_____

_____

_____

What are the Short Term Needs from an Outsource
Organization? (3 months to 1 year)

_____
_____
_____
_____
_____
_____
_____
_____
_____

What are the Long Term Needs from an Outsourcing
Organization? (1 months to 5 years)

_____
_____
_____
_____
_____
_____
_____
_____

Reflection

Reflection